Night Night Birmingham

Night Night animals at the zoo.

THE BIRMINGHAM Z

Night Night Vulcan, too.

Night Night Birmingham Museum of Art.

Night Night Railroad Park.

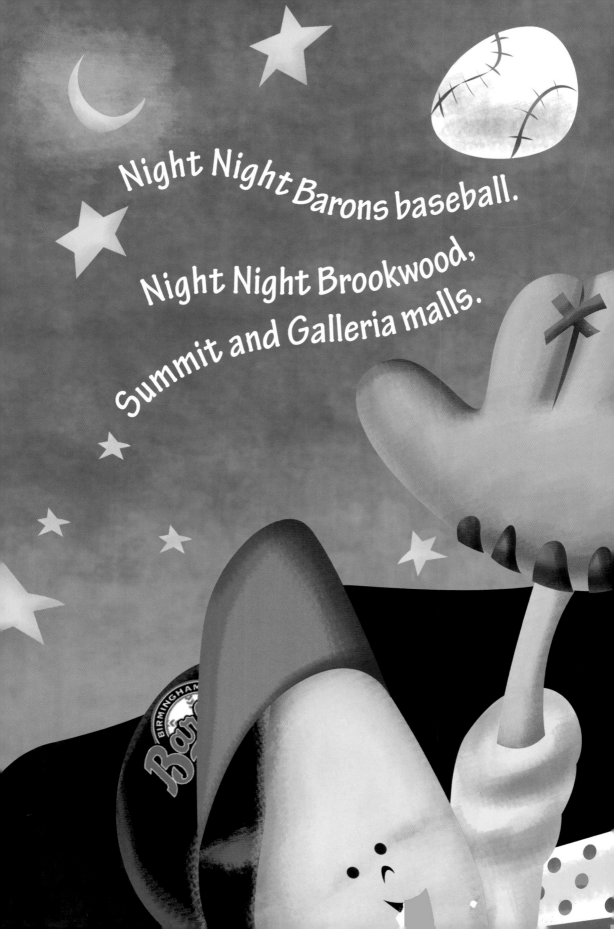

Night Night Barons baseball.

Night Night Brookwood, Summit and Galleria malls.

Night Night Barber Motorsports and cars that race.

Night Night Ruffner Mountain Nature place.

Night Night BJCC and
the stars of its shows.

Night Night Sloss Furnace where iron glows.

Night Night Botanical Gardens
and flowers in bloom.

Night Night McWane Center
and its science rooms.

Night Night schools where
students learn in class.
Night Night Civil Rights Institute
that honors the past.

Night Night downtown and twinkling lights.

Night Night neighborhoods where families sleep tight.

Night Night Mommy,
Daddy, Fido and Fluffy, too.

Night Night Birmingham,
my home, I love you.